REACHING FOR THE STARS

INVESTIGATING SPACE MYSTERIES

Mike Downs

ROURKE'S SCHOOL to HOME CONNECTIONS

BEFORE AND DURING READING ACTIVITIES

Before Reading: *Building Background Knowledge and Vocabulary*

Building background knowledge can help children process new information and build upon what they already know. Before reading a book, it is important to tap into what children already know about the topic. This will help them develop their vocabulary and increase their reading comprehension.

Questions and Activities to Build Background Knowledge:

1. Look at the front cover of the book and read the title. What do you think this book will be about?
2. What do you already know about this topic?
3. Take a book walk and skim the pages. Look at the table of contents, photographs, captions, and bold words. Did these text features give you any information or predictions about what you will read in this book?

Vocabulary: *Vocabulary Is Key to Reading Comprehension*

Use the following directions to prompt a conversation about each word.

- Read the vocabulary words.
- What comes to mind when you see each word?
- What do you think each word means?

Vocabulary Words:
- dwarf planets
- event horizon
- infrared
- light-years
- optical
- ordinary matter

During Reading: *Reading for Meaning and Understanding*

To achieve deep comprehension of a book, children are encouraged to use close reading strategies. During reading, it is important to have children stop and make connections. These connections result in deeper analysis and understanding of a book.

Close Reading a Text

During reading, have children stop and talk about the following:

- Any confusing parts
- Any unknown words
- Text-to-text, text-to-self, text-to-world connections
- The main idea in each chapter or heading

Encourage children to use context clues to determine the meaning of any unknown words. These strategies will help children learn to analyze the text more thoroughly as they read.

When you are finished reading this book, turn to the next-to-last page for **After-Reading Questions** and an **Activity**.

TABLE OF CONTENTS

Mysterious Space 4

The Amazing Things We Don't See 12

Where Are the Aliens? 18

The Size of Our Quest! 24

Our Own Galaxy 30

Index 31

After-Reading Questions 31

Activity 31

About the Author 32

MYSTERIOUS SPACE

Look at the sky on a dark, moonless night. You'll see planets and stars. You can spot satellites whizzing by. You might even see the International Space Station!

Our Milky Way galaxy looks like a river of stars. Three other galaxies are also visible to the naked eye: the Andromeda galaxy, the Large Magellanic Cloud, and the Small Magellanic Cloud. As you might guess, the last two galaxies look like clouds! But to unravel the mysteries of space, we need to see a lot more. To do that, we use telescopes.

The Horsehead Nebula

A nebula is an area where gas, dust, and other matter clump together and can become dense enough to form stars.

The earliest record of a telescope comes from the Netherlands in 1608. Galileo used one to discover four moons around Jupiter. Now we know Jupiter has at least 79 moons!

Using powerful new telescopes, astronomers have discovered asteroids, comets, and **dwarf planets**. They also noticed that Pluto wasn't like other planets. In 2006, poor Pluto lost its place as the ninth planet in the solar system. Now it's considered to be one of several dwarf planets that orbit the sun.

dwarf planets (dworf PLAN-its): round or mostly round celestial bodies that orbit the sun, are not moons, and do not have enough gravity to be full-sized planets

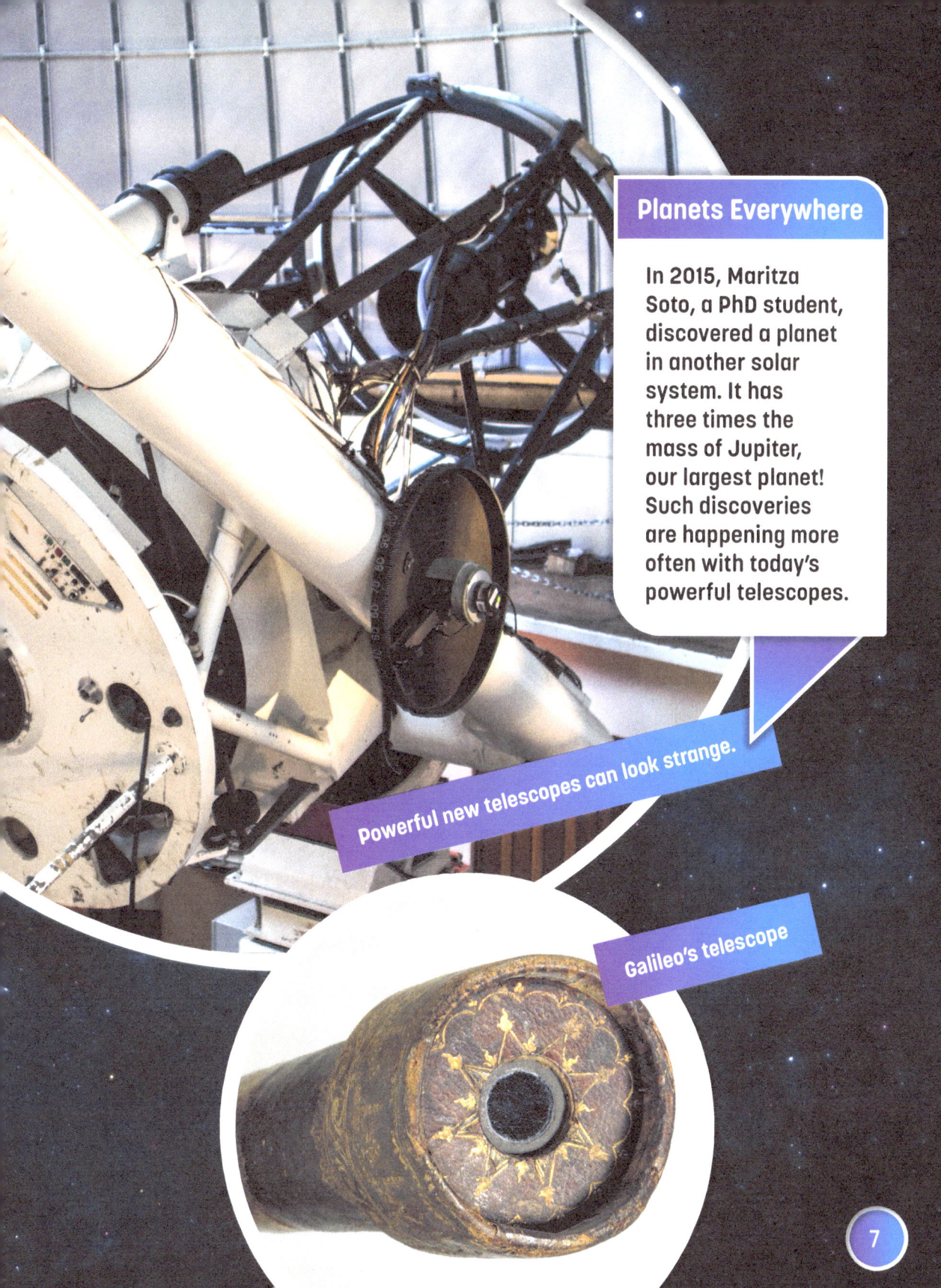

Planets Everywhere

In 2015, Maritza Soto, a PhD student, discovered a planet in another solar system. It has three times the mass of Jupiter, our largest planet! Such discoveries are happening more often with today's powerful telescopes.

Powerful new telescopes can look strange.

Galileo's telescope

Telescopes have helped astronomers make incredible discoveries. The powerful Hubble Space Telescope, spotted thousands of new galaxies during its missions. But telescopes don't display an an exact picture. Some faraway galaxies look warped and twisted. The massive gravity of a black hole or another galaxy can bend the light coming from behind it. This is called gravitational lensing.

Twisted Light

Some neutron stars have so much gravity that scientists can see part of the back of the star. This is because the light curves so much.

The Hubble Telescope maps parts of the universe.

Black holes have so much gravity that nearby light can't escape. Their name is also a little misleading. Black holes aren't really holes, but rather objects with supergravity.

Scientists think the Milky Way galaxy has millions of stellar black holes. Stellar black holes form when stars explode. Supermassive black holes are millions of times larger. Most galaxies swirl around supermassive black holes.

In 2019, researcher Katie Bouman was part of a team that created an algorithm , or step-by-step method for solving a problem, which allowed us to see the first picture of an actual black hole!

event horizon (i-VENT huh-RYE-zuhn): the boundary of a black hole that nothing can escape beyond

Galaxies circle this supermassive black hole.

Don't Get Too Close!

The edge of a black hole is called the **event horizon**. The black hole's gravity will suck in anything that gets too close to the event horizon.

THE AMAZING THINGS WE DON'T SEE

Sight is not the only way to study the universe. Scientists also study the microwave and radio wave energy our universe emits. In 1992, a radio telescope discovered the first planets outside our solar system, or exoplanets. To date, we have discovered more than 4,000 exoplanets using many different types of telescopes. In 2015, scientists detected gravitational waves from two black holes that crashed into each other. Huge crashes like that send invisible waves of gravity rippling through space.

A Long Wait

In 1916, Einstein predicted that waves of gravity existed. Some scientists didn't believe him. It took nearly 100 years before we detected the first gravitational waves to prove him right.

Looking into the night sky, we see stars, planets, and galaxies. They are made of **ordinary matter**, just like humans. But the universe is mostly made up of stuff we can't see. The emptiness of space is full of dark matter and dark energy. We know it is because we can measure its gravity and microwave energy. Scientists believe that we can see only about four percent of the universe. That means most of the weight in the universe is invisible!

ordinary matter (OR-duh-ner-ee MAT-ur): the combination of protons, neutrons, and electrons that make up the visible universe

The "Fireworks" galaxy had 10 supernovas in the last century.

Infrared telescopes help us see more of our universe. They detect the heat given off by objects. The Spitzer Infrared Space Telescope discovered a massive dusty ring around Saturn that couldn't be seen by **optical** telescopes. This ring, called Phoebe, circles the planet from millions of miles away. It's far outside the rings we can see. The Spitzer Space Telescope also discovered stars whizzing around the supermassive black hole at the center of the Milky Way galaxy.

infrared (in-FRUH-red): **beyond the visible spectrum at its red end**

optical (AHP-ti-kuhl): **of or relating to vision**

The Spitzer Space Telescope was launched in 2003.

The Phoebe dust ring

WHERE ARE THE ALIENS?

Aliens are everywhere! Well, at least in science fiction novels and movies. We haven't found aliens yet, but we're trying to! One way scientists search for alien life is by looking for water on planets and moons. Tiny organisms might live in the water. Discovering the first alien life outside of Earth, even a teeny, tiny organism, would be the thrill of a lifetime! But it wouldn't be quite as exciting as spotting a tentacled alien waving hello.

Searching for Strangers

Rosalba Bonaccorsi of the Search for Extraterrestrial Intelligence (SETI) Institute wants to pinpoint areas on planets where life might occur. The SETI Institute also searches for radio signals and laser flashes from other planets.

Radio telescopes search for alien signals.

What about the unidentified flying objects (UFOs) people see? Are those UFOs flying saucers or alien ships?

No, they aren't either. But many people do see UFOs! Most UFOs are actually balloons, flares, rockets, meteors, drones, or military experiments. Venus is also to blame. Its bright, flickering light can make it appear only miles away instead of millions of miles away.

These lenticular clouds might be mistaken for UFOs.

If aliens are similar to us, they would want to live on planets like Earth. Our solar system contains three types of planets. There are rocky planets (such as Earth and Mars), ice giants (such as Uranus and Neptune), and gas giants (such as Jupiter and Saturn).

Rocky planets are made of rocks and metals. Ice giants are huge planets made of heavy elements, such as sulfur, nitrogen, carbon, and oxygen. Gas giants are mostly gases, such as helium and hydrogen, with no ground at all. A rocket would sink right to the center of a gas giant. You wouldn't want to volunteer for *that* trip!

Jupiter is a gas giant, the fifth planet from the sun and the largest in our solar system.

Saturn
Mars
Neptune
Venus
Sun
Earth
Mercury
Jupiter
Uranus

23

THE SIZE OF OUR QUEST!

Our universe is so vast; it's almost impossible to understand. The fastest rocket we could ever build would go nearly the speed of light. At that speed, it would take about 4.3 years to reach the nearest star system, Alpha Centauri. Rockets today can't go that fast. Using the fastest rocket ever launched to date, it would take about 6,850 years.

Speedy Rays

Light is the fastest thing in the universe. But how fast is light? It's so fast it can circle Earth 7.5 times per second.

Alpha Centauri contains the closest stars in the Milky Way galaxy. The Milky Way itself is only a tiny speck in the universe, and recent research shows it might measure 200,000 light-years across. There are possibly 100 to 200 billion galaxies. Every galaxy is chock full of mystery and the unknown. To see those mysteries firsthand, we'll have to figure out a way to travel at a speed faster than light.

light-years (lite-yeerz): units of length in astronomy equal to the distance that light travels in one year

On the Move

A wormhole connecting one part of the universe to another is possible, in theory. Unfortunately, it would probably self-destruct if it were used. Scientists might want to work on that problem before flying into one.

For now, even with all of our telescopes, rockets, and space probes, we can only study the tiniest bit of outer space. Think of it as trying to draw a picture of New York City while looking through a straw. Every time you move your straw, you see something exciting and new.

It's the same with our universe. With every advance in technology, scientists make fascinating discoveries and theories change. New planets, stars, nebulae, and galaxies are discovered. But there are still millions of discoveries to be made and countless mysteries to be solved. What amazing secrets will you uncover?

Our Own Galaxy

This map of our solar system shows planets, the asteroid belt, and Pluto. They are all squished together to fit. On a map with the proper scale, if the sun was less than ½ inch around, the orbit of Neptune would be about a football field distance away.

Asteroids

Pluto Dwarf Planet

Index

aliens 18, 22
black holes 10, 11, 12
gas giant(s) 22, 23
gravitational lensing 8, 30
nebula(e) 5, 28

Pluto 6, 30
telescope(s) 4, 6, 7, 8, 9, 12, 16, 19, 28
wormhole 27

After-Reading Questions

1. Which galaxies can we see without using a telescope?
2. What happened to Pluto in 2006?
3. What happens to light when it passes near an object with massive gravity? What is this called?
4. What does the SETI Institute do? What methods do they use to search?
5. Name some of the common objects that people describe as UFOs.

Activity

There are three main types of planets: rocky planets, gas giants, and ice giants. Draw these three types of planets. Then, think about what type of alien might be able to live on each planet. Draw a picture of each alien near its home planet.

About the Author

Mike Downs enjoys writing books for young readers. He especially loves writing about outer space. If he ever has a chance to ride in a rocket ship, he'll do it! Until then, he has to write from his desk at home.

© 2022 Rourke Educational Media

All rights reserved. No part of this book may be reproduced or utilized in any form or by any means, electronic or mechanical including photocopying, recording, or by any information storage and retrieval system without permission in writing from the publisher.

www.rourkeeducationalmedia.com

PHOTO CREDITS: Cover, pages 4-8, 10-16, 18, 20, 22-24, 26-28, 30, 31: ©Cappan/ Getty Images; cover: ©KTSDesign/SCIENCEPHOTOLIBRARY/Newscom; cover, 1, 3, 6, 8, 14, 16, 18, 20, 24, 326: ©LineTale/ Shutterstock.com; pages 4-5: ©Udo Kieslich; page 5: ©DeepSkyTXI; pages 6-7: ©Daniel Oberhaus/ Licensed under Creative Commons Attribution-Share Alike 4.0 International; page 7: ©Fine Art Images Heritage Images/Newscom; pages 8-9: ©Stocktrek Images/ Getty Images; pages10-11: ©NASA/ZUMA Press/Newscom; page 11: ©Elena11/ Shutterstock.com; pages 12-13: ©Mytida/ Shutterstock.com; pages 14-15: ©ESA/ Hubble & NASA, A. Leroy, K.S. Long; page 15: ©NASA/JPL-Caltech; pages 14-15: ©Vladi333/ Shutterstock.com; pages 14-15: ©NASA/JPL-Caltech/Keck; pages 18-19: ©Paulo Afonso/ Shutterstock.com; pages 20-21: ©Dmitry Dubikovskiy/ZUMA Press/Newscom; pages 22-23: ©NASA/JPL-Caltech/SwRI/MSSS/Kevin M. Gill; page 23: ©SiberianArt/ Getty Images; pages 24-25: ©NASA/ESA/UPI/Newscom; pages 26-27: ©Rost9/ Shutterstock.com; pages 28-29: ©Cylonphoto/ Getty Images page 29: ©Alexyz3d/ Getty Images; page 30: ©Zonda/ Shutterstock.com; page 30: ©Jurik Peter/ Shutterstock.com; page 30: ©Irina Dmitrienko/Newscom

Edited by: Jennifer Doyle
Cover and interior design by: Alison Tracey

Library of Congress PCN Data

Investigating Space Mysteries / Mike Downs
(Reaching for the Stars)
ISBN 978-1-73164-935-5 (hard cover)(alk. paper)
ISBN 978-1-73164-883-9 (soft cover)
ISBN 978-1-73164-987-4 (e-Book)
ISBN 9781731650399 (ePub)
Library of Congress Control Number: 2021935276

Rourke Educational Media
Printed in the United States of America
03-0202313053